The Quest to End World Hunger

CHARITY & PHILANTHROPY
UNLEASHED

Marylou
Morano
Kjelle

Mitchell Lane
PUBLISHERS
P.O. Box 196
Hockessin, DE 19707

Mitchell Lane
PUBLISHERS

CHARITY & PHILANTHROPY UNLEASHED

Conquering Disease
Emergency Aid
Environmental Protection
Helping Children with Life-Threatening Medical Issues
Helping Our Veterans
Preserving Human Rights Around the World
The Quest to End World Hunger
Support for Education

PUBLISHER'S NOTE: The facts in this book have been thoroughly researched. Documentation of such research can be found on pages 44–45. While every possible effort has been made to ensure accuracy, the publisher will not assume liability for damages caused by inaccuracies in the data, and makes no warranty on the accuracy of the information contained herein.

The Internet sites referenced herein were active as of the publication date. Due to the fleeting nature of some web sites, we cannot guarantee that they will all be active when you are reading this book.

Printing 1 2 3 4 5 6 7 8 9

Library of Congress
Cataloging-in-Publication Data

Kjelle, Marylou Morano.
  The quest to end world hunger / Marylou Morano Kjelle.
    pages cm. — (Charity and philanthropy unleashed)
  Audience: Grades 4 to 8.
  Includes bibliographical references and index.
  ISBN 978-1-61228-570-2 (library bound)
  1. Food relief—Juvenile literature.
  2. Agricultural assistance—Juvenile literature.
  3. Charities—Juvenile literature. I. Title.
  HV696.F6K577 2015
  363.8'5 — dc23
                                                        2014008299

eBook ISBN: 9781612286082

                                                        PBP

Contents

Introduction

Most people will never experience the sensation of hunger that comes from going for long periods of time with little or nothing to eat. But malnutrition, which is defined as not eating enough nutritious food to maintain a healthy lifestyle, is the world's number-one health risk. Food insecurity, the condition of not always knowing where the next meal will come from, is a reality for many people, both in wealthy countries like the United States and in developing countries. Each day, more than fifteen thousand people die because they didn't get enough food to eat.[1] Food insecurity causes a number of conditions ranging from hunger to malnutrition to starvation. The Food and Agriculture Organization (FAO), an agency under the direction of the United Nations, works all over the world to bring high-quality food to people who are food-insecure. The FAO estimates that of the world's 7 billion people, 1.3 billion face some form of food insecurity.[2] Included in this number are 20 million children under the age of five who are severely malnourished.[3]

As strange as it may sound, producing more food isn't the answer to ending hunger. There is already enough food in the world today to satisfy the nutritional needs of everyone living on Earth. If this is the case, then why is one in every six people facing food insecurity? Another United Nations organization, the World Food Programme (WFP) is the world's largest humanitarian agency working to eradicate hunger in the world.[4] The WFP lists six reasons for hunger: poverty, a lack of investment in agriculture, extreme climate and weather conditions, war or other conflict, rising food prices, and food wastage.[5] In some countries, hunger may be the result of a combination of several of these factors.

The statistics on hunger are staggering, but there is also a bit of good news. In the last twenty years, the total number of undernourished people in the world has fallen 17 percent, even as the population of the world has grown by more than 30 percent.[6] This is due, in great part, to the many charities and philanthropies working throughout the world to eradicate hunger. A philanthropy is a humanitarian organization that places helping others ahead of earning a financial profit. For this reason, a philanthropy is often referred to as a nonprofit organization. A philanthropy relies on others, like private individuals, corporations, and other philanthropies, for the resources it needs to do its work. A philanthropy is a politically neutral organization that does not get involved in the affairs of the countries in which it works. Because it has no government affiliation, a philanthropy is also referred to as a non-governmental organization (NGO). Charities are similar organizations, but they tend to focus on short-term fixes, while philanthropies work to create long-term solutions to problems.

Philanthropies and charities are working to wipe out hunger throughout the world in many ways. They are teaching people modern farming techniques that result in more plentiful harvests. They are working with communities to establish safe and clean supplies of water. They are helping people, especially women, start their own businesses. This will raise their incomes and allow them to purchase more nutritious food for those they care for. They are also creating programs to feed hungry children, both here in the United States and abroad. They are getting high-quality, nutritious food and water to people who are without because of a natural disaster, like an earthquake or hurricane.

In September 2000, world leaders from 189 countries met in New York at the Millennium Summit, sponsored by the United Nations. After this meeting, the Millennium Development Goals were created. These were a set of eight goals that the leaders committed to meeting by 2015. As part of their pledge to "eradicate extreme poverty and hunger," leaders aimed to "halve, between 1990 and 2015, the proportion of people who suffer from hunger."[7] Undernourished people represented 23.6 percent of the world's population in 1990. Based on recent data, that number is expected to decrease to about 13 percent by 2015—a little more than half of the 1990 figure.[8] Government leaders, along with charities and philanthropies, continue to work hard not only toward this goal, but toward a day when there are no hungry people at all.

CHAPTER 1

Hunger in the United States

Every morning is the same for eleven-year-old Munaj. As he is awakened by a gentle nudge from his mother, he feels the tightness in his stomach that reminds him he didn't eat very much for dinner last night. Munaj dresses quickly in his school uniform—a pair of khaki pants and a green polo shirt—and heads to the small table that is in a corner of his family's two-room living quarters. His older sister and his younger brother are already at the table watching his mother prepare their morning meal. First, Munaj's mother pours each child a glass of milk, which she has made by mixing water with a white powder that came out of a can. It doesn't taste like the milk in the carton, but Munaj drinks it anyway, pretending it is the free milk that he gets for lunch at school.

Munaj's mother then takes a banana and cuts it into quarters; she gives a piece to each child and keeps one for herself. Next she peels an orange and divides the juicy segments among the children. She skips her own portion this time, so that each of the children can have an extra piece of the fruit, which is full of vitamins. Munaj knows that his mother is just as hungry as he is, but a few cups of the free coffee that she will drink at work will help quiet her own hunger pains.

As Munaj and his siblings eat their breakfast, all he can think about is food. Because his mother doesn't have a large income, Munaj and his siblings qualify for free lunch at school. This is a program sponsored by the United States government that tries to meet the nutritional needs of school-age kids by providing a nourishing lunch. For dinner, Munaj will probably have a peanut

Each day over thirty-one million school children receive a nourishing lunch either free of charge or at low cost thanks to the National School Lunch Program sponsored by the United States government.

Many families in the United States don't earn enough to pay for shelter, clothing, health care, and nourishing food. Food pantries help families in need by providing non-perishable foods and other staples at no cost. The food is donated by members of the community, corporations, and organizations.

butter sandwich and a chocolate chip cookie. Munaj's mother didn't buy the cookies—the family has no money for such treats. They came from a package that was in a bag of food that Munaj's mother picked up at the community food pantry the day before. Munaj knows that the single package of cookies will last his family of four one week, and for this he feels fortunate. Some of his friends have larger families, and one package of cookies shared by many more people won't last as long.[1]

Munaj and the other children living in his community are always hungry. They go to school hungry. They go to bed hungry. They are hungry before they eat a meal and they are still hungry afterward because the meal did not contain enough calories to satisfy them.

Based on what you've read, where would you guess that Munaj lives? Would you say a sub-Saharan country in Africa, like Somalia? Or a country in Asia, like Bangladesh? Perhaps you would say Munaj lives in a Caribbean country like Haiti? If your answer was any of these countries, you would be wrong. Munaj and his family live in a poverty-stricken community within one of the largest cities in the United States.

Many Americans maintain a high standard of living. They have homes and cars, and jobs that provide salaries to help pay for all they need and even some extras, like vacations and large-screen televisions. This lifestyle has given America its reputation of being a land of plenty. Although it is the richest country in the world, one in every six people who lives in the United States is not sure where his or her next meal will come from. That includes almost sixteen million American children who live in food-insecure households.[2] Like Munaj, many of these children are not homeless or living on the street. They are part of a family unit where at least one caretaker has a job. But this income isn't enough to pay for all the family's necessities, like food, shelter, and clothing. An unexpected emergency, like a broken bone or an illness, may force a family's caretaker to choose between being seen by a doctor and putting food on the table. There may not be enough money for both, and going to the doctor's office may force a family to give up one or two meals. It is even possible that the family may have to go without food altogether for several days.

One domestic charity working to eradicate hunger in the United States is Feeding America. This organization works with established federal agencies, such as the Emergency Food Assistance Program (TEFAP). TEFAP provides food to Feeding America's food banks, food pantries, and soup kitchens.[3] Feeding America also works with another federal program, the Commodity Supplemental Food Program (CSFP), which provides foods like peanut butter, beans, tuna, juices, and other nutritious foods to about 595,000 low-income Americans each month.[4] This number includes many Americans over sixty years old who live on a fixed income and don't always have enough money to purchase food. Working with a network of over two hundred food banks nationwide, Feeding America and its partners serve thirty-seven million people annually.[5] In addition, Feeding America sends food, water, and volunteers to areas that have been devastated by a natural disaster, such as an earthquake or hurricane.

Getting healthier food into our schools and communities has always been of concern to First Lady Michelle Obama. One of the ways she shows her commitment to eradicating hunger is by preparing bags of non-perishable food items for distribution at the Capital Area Food Bank for Feeding America.

Share Our Strength is another organization dedicated to ending hunger, especially childhood hunger, both in the United States and throughout the world. Share Our Strength was started in 1984 in the basement of a house in Washington, DC, by siblings Bill and Debbie Shore. The Shores were inspired to establish the charity when a famine occurred in Ethiopia in 1984 and 1985. It was Bill and Debbie's belief that everyone has a strength to share in the global fight against hunger and poverty. Today, one of Share Our Strength's goals is to make childhood hunger a national priority in the United States.[6]

In 2006, Share Our Strength launched a campaign called No Kid Hungry. The goal of this project is to end childhood hunger in America by seeing that all children get the healthy food they need every day. In addition, Share Our Strength holds classes, called Cooking Matters, where families can learn to both shop for and cook healthy and economical meals.

These charities, and others like them, are helping to keep American kids well nourished and healthy, all year long.

School's Out, but Food's In!

Federal programs provide more than 31 million children free or reduced-cost meals during the school year. However, only 2.3 million children receive these meals when school is out for summer vacation.[7] Sponsorship by large corporations like American Express and Kraft Foods, as well as private citizens and community leaders, helps Share our Strength provide meals to hungry American children even when school is not in session.[8] Another organization, the YMCA, with help from the Walmart Foundation, also keeps kids eighteen and younger from getting hungry during the summer break. The YMCA has established more than nine hundred summer food program sites nationwide. This translates into providing four million healthy summertime meals and snacks to one hundred thousand kids. But the Y isn't only about feeding kids in the summer. During the school year, the YMCA serves nutritious food to kids who attend its afterschool program at any of 1,400 sites throughout the United States.[9] Feeding America also helps keep kids from getting hungry when school is out. Its BackPack Program sends backpacks filled with nutritious and easy-to-prepare food home with kids on weekends and school breaks.[10]

Celebrities like actress Marcia Cross work to help fight childhood hunger. In 2009, she attended the launch of Feeding America's BackPack Program at St. Aloysius School in New York City.

CHAPTER 2

Fighting Famine

Hunger has most likely always been a part of the history of humans. Prehistoric hunters and gatherers were aware that the changes in seasons signaled a change in the availability and variety of food, whether it was plant, animal, or fish. Severe food shortages, however, most likely didn't arise until early human societies shifted to farming communities, and weather, soil conditions, pests, and water availability affected their ability to grow food. The earliest written accounts of famines were recorded on Egyptian stone pillars called stelae.[1] Europeans experienced frequent food shortages during the Middle Ages, the roughly one thousand years between the fifth and fifteenth centuries. Later, one well-known famine, called the Great Irish Potato Famine, began in Ireland in the late summer of 1845 and lasted for six years. An airborne fungus carried into the country on cargo ships infected the country's main source of food, the potato, causing the crop to fail. The shortage of food that resulted caused more than one million people to die of starvation.[2]

More recently, in 2011 a severe drought combined with rising food prices and a war in the African country of Somalia caused a famine in the East African peninsula called the Horn of Africa. The famine killed tens of thousands and left millions more hungry.[3] Save the Children, an international philanthropy dedicated to helping children, was one of many humanitarian agencies that provided relief to the area.

Save the Children was founded by two sisters, Eglantyne Jebb and Dorothy Buxton, in England after World War I. The two were concerned about the children who lived in the areas of Central

Young men in Burundi unload sacks of food aid from the World Food Programme.

Although the Save the Children was started almost a century ago, it is still providing help to those in need. Well-known people, such as Samantha Cameron, the wife of British Prime Minister David Cameron, call attention to the great work the philanthropy is doing by visiting sites where Save the Children works, like this refugee settlement in Lebanon, close to the Syrian border.

Europe that had been devastated by the war. Eglantyne was an activist and a reformer—two traits not often found in a woman born in Victorian England. In fact, the Save the Children Fund received its first donation as a result of Eglantyne's imprisonment. In 1919 she was arrested in Trafalgar Square for protesting a post-WWI British blockade that prevented food from getting to children in Austria and Germany. Since she did not have the government's permission to distribute leaflets, she was arrested, found guilty, and fined £5.[4] Sir Archibald Bodkin, a lawyer, publicly supported Eglantyne by giving her a £5 note (about $300 in today's US dollars) to pay the fine. Eglantyne took the money and donated it to a new fund she was starting to help the starving children. Eglantyne called her new fund the Save the Children Fund.

Eglantyne and Dorothy's efforts to start the Save the Children Fund were at first met with resistance. At a public meeting at Royal Albert Hall, spectators threw fruit at the sisters and called them traitors because they wanted to help the children who lived in enemy countries. Eglantyne used her powers of persuasion to convince the spectators to donate to her new philanthropy. That very evening £10,000 (about $600,000 in today's US dollars) was raised. Within ten days, food and other aid purchased with the money was on its way to Vienna, the capital of Austria. Later, donations were used to help children in France, Belgium, the Balkans, Hungary, and Turkey.[5]

When she began Save the Children, Eglantyne thought it would be a temporary agency that would take care of the short-term emergency of the starving children. But the agency acquired a reputation for the efficient way it helped those in need. Soon it was being called upon to help with other disasters, like the 1921 famine in Russia, where it launched an operation to feed 650,000 people—for a shilling (about $3 in today's US dollars) per person, per week.[6] In 1932, a group of social activists opened a Save the Children office in the United States. Among the first to be helped were children living in Kentucky, Tennessee, North Carolina, Mississippi, and Missouri. Following World War II, Save the

A group of British schoolchildren took the worldwide hunger problem into their own hands when they presented Prime Minister David Cameron with these hand-decorated plates on June 6, 2013. They created the plates to bring attention to the Enough Food for Everyone IF campaign. Two days later, the UK committed to spending an additional £375 million (US $630 million) to fight child malnutrition over the next seven years.

Children expanded even further to help children in Yugoslavia, Poland, and Greece.

Today, Save the Children has an eight-step plan of action for dealing with child hunger in the world. The plan includes things like fortifying basic foods with extra nutrients, giving poor mothers money or vouchers so they can buy food for their families, and getting life-saving food supplies to children quickly when there is a natural disaster. In January 2013, together with more than two hundred other charities, Save the Children launched the Enough Food for Everyone IF campaign. This initiative's goal is to make food available to anyone by working to "increase investment and improve the transparency, accountability, and governance of key aspects of the food system."[7] As a result of the nine-month campaign, governments, companies, and charities pledged $4 billion toward the fight against hunger. The money will be used to fund projects to combat malnutrition in the world's most poverty-stricken countries. Save the Children estimates that Enough Food for Everyone IF will save 1.7 million lives.[8]

UNICEF

The Horn of Africa famine affected more than thirteen million people[9] living in the countries of Ethiopia, Somalia, Kenya, Sudan, South Sudan, and Djibouti. The United Nations Children's Fund (UNICEF) was one of the principal agencies helping victims during the Horn of Africa famine. UNICEF works in more than 190 countries around the world to save and improve children's lives. In addition to battling hunger, UNICEF also provides health care, clean water, education, immunization, and other services.

UNICEF was created in 1946 by the United Nations to provide food, clothing, and health care to the many European children facing famine and disease as a result of the end of World War II. Today, UNICEF is committed to preventing and treating child malnutrition by helping children around the globe obtain the nutrition needed for a healthy and promising future. One of UNICEF's goals is to see a day when zero children die from preventable causes, including malnutrition. To fulfill its mission, UNICEF partners with celebrity ambassadors, NGOs, corporations, volunteers, and financial donors. Since 1960, UNICEF has helped reduce the worldwide child mortality rate by more than 60 percent.[10]

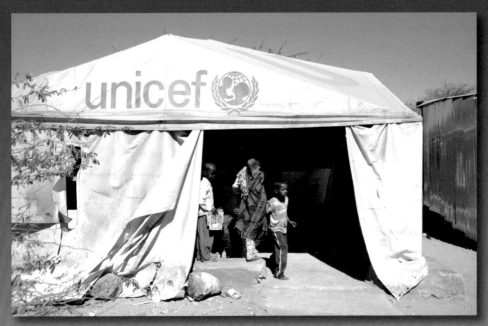

Children gather at a UNICEF school in a refugee camp in the outskirts of Hargeisa, Somaliland.

CHAPTER 3

Helping Women Fight Hunger

Based in New York City, The Hunger Project is an international philanthropy founded in 1977 to end hunger wherever it is found in the world. The organization approaches hunger as just one part of a network of related issues that includes employment, health, education, environmental balance, and social justice. The Hunger Project believes that these concerns must be addressed collectively for any single one to be solved permanently, and it utilizes more than 385,000 trained volunteers who work all over the world to lift people out of hunger and poverty.[1]

Because of its well-rounded approach to hunger, The Hunger Project sees itself as more of a strategic organization than a relief organization. This means that in addition to getting food to people in need, The Hunger Project works to eliminate the root causes of hunger. The agency gets involved in the planning and implementation of policies and tactics to end hunger. Delivering food to those who need it is important, but teaching people how to obtain their own food is more helpful in the long run. The Hunger Project remains flexible in order to meet the changing challenges of eliminating hunger.

Shortly after it was founded, The Hunger Project used public education and advocacy to ask the global community for a commitment to end hunger. The Hunger Project went on to work in Cambodia and Somalia, and eventually the entire African continent. The group recognized that in some areas, hunger was the result of poor leadership. This was the case in Africa in the 1980s, so The Hunger Project created a prize for African leadership to encourage the committed, effective leadership so greatly

Ellen Johnson Sirleaf, president of Liberia, accepts the 2001 Africa Prize. This prize was created in the 1980s to encourage African leaders to create solutions to hunger in their countries.

Developing countries such as Somalia are hardest hit by poverty, war, and drought. Often considered the lowest-ranking members of society, women are also usually the ones who have to find ways to feed their families.

needed at the time. The most effective leaders help their people make improvements not only to feed the hungry, but to prevent hunger by improving health, education, nutrition, and family income as well.

Currently, The Hunger Project works in Africa, Latin America, and South Asia.[2] But whatever country The Hunger Project is in, it approaches its work in three ways. These are: organizing people at the grassroots level to build self-reliance; empowering women to become key agents for change; and creating partnerships with local governments to see that leaders provide access to resources and information, and are accountable to their citizens.[3]

Women are often the ones responsible for growing, finding, and preparing food for their families. Therefore, according to The Hunger Project, women play a key role in ridding the world of hunger. The organization believes it can best lift a community out of poverty and hunger by helping all members become self-reliant, or able to satisfy their own needs. Throughout the world, most of the poorest people are women.[4] It is especially important for mothers to become self-reliant because the health and well-being of a child is linked to how well a mother is able to care for herself.

Many cultures throughout the world undervalue women and the contributions they make to the family and society. In addition, women who live in poorer, developing countries are often controlled by laws and rules set by the men of the community. This can translate into women not getting their fair share of whatever food (and other resources) are available. According to The Hunger Project, this control of women and unfair allocation of food gives rise to a deadly cycle of malnutrition that begins when a baby girl is born. This cycle is seen often in South Asian countries, like Bangladesh and India. South Asia has the highest rates of child malnutrition in the world.[5] The babies born in these countries are frequently underweight and malnourished when they are born. Since South Asian women and girls are not valued as highly as the men and boys in their families, a female infant

In South Asian nations like India, girls and women are not considered as valuable as boys and men. Because of this, when resources like food are scarce, the women and girls are the first to go without.

may not receive as much nutritious food as her brother. She may be fed less food, less often. As she grows older, a girl usually does not have the same access to health care and education as her male siblings. In addition, South Asian women often get married and become pregnant when they are teenagers. Without

enough food and proper nutrition during pregnancy, a woman's baby is more likely to be malnourished, which means he or she is more susceptible to illness. This cycle repeats itself and is difficult to break.[6]

The Hunger Project is also assisting hunger-prone women in Africa in several ways. In 1999, the philanthropy began its Microfinance Program. In Africa women grow the majority of food eaten by their families. Although entire communities rely on the food grown by female farmers, these women have never had the opportunity to learn the new farming techniques that could improve their harvests. The Microfinance Program helps tens of thousands of African women farmers learn new farming techniques. The women are taught how to market and sell their excess harvest. They can also borrow small amounts of money to purchase equipment and materials which will increase their harvest. This way, they are not only feeding their own families, they are also helping to feed the community, all the while earning an income for their labors.[7]

Throughout the world, illiteracy rates are higher among women and the majority of children who do not go to school are girls.[8] Freedom from Hunger, a philanthropy based in Davis, California, also works to help women become self-sufficient. The organization offers a program called Credit with Education whereby small loans combined with education help improve the lives of poor women who live in rural areas of developing countries. Working in groups, women receive and pay back loans together. Credit with Education teaches subjects ranging from health to money management using stories, role-playing, demonstrations, discussions, and songs. Because of this teaching style, even a woman who cannot read or write can take part. The program started in 1989 with fifty women in Mali and fifty women in Thailand. Today 1.6 million women in seventeen countries take part in Credit with Education.

Over and over, Freedom from Hunger has shown that women who take part in the program earn more money and have more financial assets than women who do not. Participants are also better able to make decisions, and have better-nourished and healthier children.[9]

CARE

CARE is another leading humanitarian organization fighting hunger and global poverty. CARE was founded in 1945, after World War II left millions of people in Europe and other places in danger of starvation. Twenty-two American organizations shipped CARE packages to hungry survivors. The original CARE packages were US Army surplus parcels that contained enough food to provide one meal to ten soldiers. Americans could send the packages to their friends and family in war-torn countries. The contents of a typical CARE package included beans, meats, margarine, lard, fruit preserves, honey, raisins, sugar, egg powder, chocolate, coffee, and milk powder. The packages, which cost Americans $10, were guaranteed to reach the recipients in Europe within four months. Even President Harry S. Truman sent CARE packages overseas. Most packages were sent to specific people at specific addresses, but some were sent to unnamed addressees, like "a school teacher in Germany."

Today CARE is involved in nearly one thousand projects that fight hunger and poverty in eighty-four countries. Like The Hunger Project and Freedom from Hunger, CARE has special programs designed to help poor women. CARE's community-based efforts are geared towards helping women by working to increase basic literacy skills and prevent violence against women. The organization also works to provide and improve women's health care and nutrition and increase their access to clean water and sanitation.[10]

Rwandans carry bundles of food home from a CARE distribution. CARE stands for Cooperative for Assistance and Relief Everywhere.

CHAPTER 4

Ending Hunger with Sustainable Agriculture

One way to end hunger once and for all is by bringing sustainable, or long-term, agricultural techniques to countries with rural economies. This method of solving the hunger crisis involves the cooperation of the people at risk and requires them to participate in the solution to the problems that cause their hunger. In most cases, this involves teaching people how to become independent growers of food, so that they are able to provide for their own nutritional needs. Learning to care for oneself and one's family is one of the best ways to break the cycle of hunger and the poverty that almost always accompanies it.

Farming in Africa has its own challenges. Farmers face a lack of good seeds, arable soil, and adequate water supplies. It is almost impossible to get financing for improving their farms, and the governments often do not support their efforts.[1] But when managed properly, African agriculture can be a powerful tool that can be used to transform and grow the African economy.

In 1997 Bill Gates, a cofounder of Microsoft, and his wife Melinda formed the Bill & Melinda Gates Foundation. One of the foundation's many goals is to alleviate poverty and hunger using multiple strategies. Partnering with the Rockefeller Foundation, the Gates Foundation formed the Alliance for a Green Revolution in Africa (AGRA) in 2006. Together with governments, corporations, and private citizens, AGRA works to help small-scale farmers grow their farms in ways that can be sustained over the long term.

Helping people to become self-sufficient by growing their own food is one of the best ways to eliminate hunger in the world. Many charities and philanthropies are teaching people sustainable agricultural methods.

CEO of Kenya-based Western Seed Company Saleem Esmail (left) shows new types of hybrid maize to AGRA chairman Kofi Annan (center) and his wife Nane (right). New types of seeds could produce more food to alleviate hunger. Some people worry, though, that genetically modified crops (known as GMOs) have not been studied enough to determine whether they are safe.

AGRA's purpose is to "fulfill the vision that Africa can feed itself and the world."[2] To achieve this, AGRA uses a variety of programs. One of these programs provides farmers with seeds that produce more food. The crops these seeds yield are also resistant to pests and diseases. Along with the Seed Program,

ENDING HUNGER WITH SUSTAINABLE AGRICULTURE

AGRA operates a Soil Health Program, which provides fertilizers to farmers, and teaches them how to use the fertilizers. AGRA's Market Access Program helps small farmers sell surplus crops, while its Policy and Advocacy Program works with governments to develop policies that support these farmers' efforts.

Rural farmers and other small business owners often don't have the credit they need to borrow money to grow their businesses. Oxfam International is a philanthropy based in the United Kingdom that helps business owners in developing countries manage their finances within their communities. The Oxford Committee for Famine Relief was formed in 1942 to help hungry people affected by World War II. In 1995, it became Oxfam International, with the mission of reducing poverty and injustice throughout the world. Today there are seventeen Oxfam affiliates, located in countries around the world including Oxfam America in the United States.

Oxfam America developed a program called Saving for Change which allows participants to loan money to each other in an organized way. Members of a group save a small amount of money each week, and lend that money to group members who are starting new businesses or need to purchase equipment or supplies to grow their current businesses. They can borrow this money at a lower interest rate than they would pay on a loan from a bank, credit union, or microfinance institution. Through these loans, women can increase their incomes, making it easier for them to provide food for themselves and their families. Without this program, these women might not receive financing for new business ventures. As an added benefit, savings groups bring community members together so they can work on other problems facing their community, like health care or agriculture projects.[3]

Oxfam America also believes in educating people about poverty and hunger and their root causes. For more than forty years, Oxfam America has used its Fast for a World Harvest program as a way of getting the word out. Those who participate

Oxfam International consists of seventeen organizations in ninety countries that work together to fight poverty. One of the places Oxfam is making a difference is South Sudan, where people like this cattle rancher (left) are helped on the local level.

in Fast for a World Harvest skip a meal and donate the money they save to Oxfam America.

Another way Oxfam America is promoting awareness of hunger is with its Hunger Banquet. At one of these events, a participant chooses a slip of paper that determines what he or she eats and where he or she sits. This is designed to demonstrate that most people have no control over their circumstances; someone can just as easily be born into poverty as they can into affluence.[4] All across the country, groups and individuals are taking action to end poverty and hunger by becoming involved with the Fast for a World Harvest program or attending Hunger Banquets.

Farmers in the United States, especially family farmers, have fallen on tough times as well. In recent years they have had difficulty accessing new markets where they can sell their food. Large farms owned by corporations usually use the newest farming techniques that produce larger harvests; make farming more profitable; and help farms survive environmental changes, like droughts, which impact yields. But it can be a challenge for smaller farmers to afford the new technologies they need to compete with the large farms.

Family-farm-centered agriculture has two impacts on hunger. First, most family farms are sources of food for the families running the farms and working the land. When a family farm fails, the farmer and his or her family are at risk of becoming food-insecure. Second, family farms usually offer their surplus directly to the community, often at prices that are better than those found at chain supermarkets and other large stores. When a family-owned farm fails, the community loses this source of fresh, nutritious food; this puts others at risk of food insecurity. In addition, the farmer loses the income that would have been obtained from the sale of the surplus food products.

In 1985, entertainers Willie Nelson, Neil Young, and John Mellencamp organized Farm Aid, a concert to help American family farmers and bring awareness of the plight of farmers to

Family farms in the United States have fallen on hard times in recent years. This impacts not only the family that owns the farm, but the community that depends on the farm's excess to supply its food.

the American public. Since then, Farm Aid has raised more than $45 million to help family farms survive and thrive.[5] One way Farm Aid raises money is by selling tickets to its annual concert.

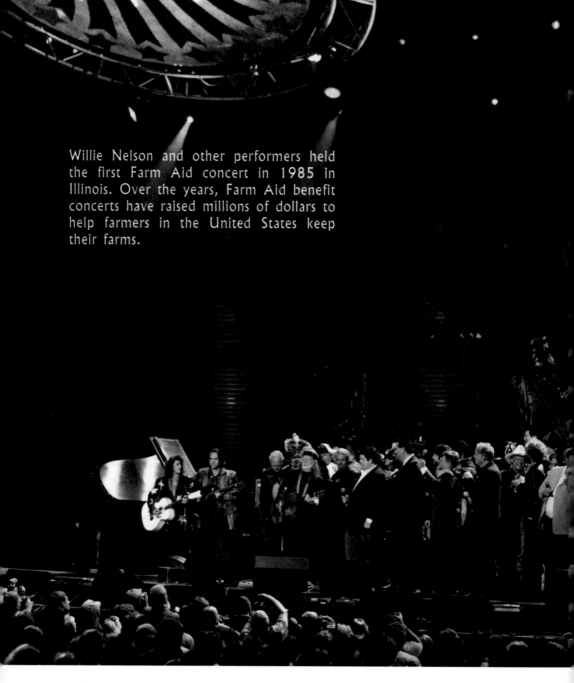

Willie Nelson and other performers held the first Farm Aid concert in 1985 in Illinois. Over the years, Farm Aid benefit concerts have raised millions of dollars to help farmers in the United States keep their farms.

The three artists from the original 1985 concert continue to perform each year, joined by Dave Matthews and other nationally-known entertainers.

Doctors Without Borders

Doctors Without Borders (also known as Médecins Sans Frontières, or MSF) is an international medical humanitarian organization created by doctors and journalists in France in 1971. Today Doctors Without Borders works in seventy countries to provide assistance to people experiencing a crisis, including malnutrition. Help is provided based on need, not gender, race, religion, or political affiliation. Doctors Without Borders estimates that twenty million children suffer from severe acute malnutrition, but only 3 percent of those children receive treatment.[6] The philanthropy is working to see that malnourished children receive more than merely a fortified cereal blend of corn and soy that may relieve a young child's hunger but does not provide proper nourishment. Such cereal does not meet the minimal nutritional needs of babies and children. According to Doctors Without Borders, one way to provide good nutrition to malnourished children is to give them Ready to Use Therapeutic Food (RUTF). This nutrition, which is in the form of a peanut butter paste, can be distributed to a large number of people at the same time. RUTF doesn't need to be mixed with water, which reduces the chance that it might become accidentally contaminated with bacteria that is present in the water. In addition to peanut butter, RUTF contains dried skimmed milk and vitamins and minerals. It can be eaten on its own or with other food. RUTF is now being produced in several African countries, such as Congo, Ethiopia, Malawi, and Niger.[7]

The effects of malnourishment are worse for the most vulnerable in a society, like the very old and the very young. A child suffering from severe malnutrition in South Sudan receives assistance from a member of the staff in a medical camp run by international humanitarian organization Doctors Without Borders.

CHAPTER 5

A World without Hunger

While hunger tends to occur in developing countries, countries at war, or those experiencing a natural disaster, no one is truly immune from hunger. An unexpected change in circumstances, like the loss of a job or being unable to work due to illness, can put any person at risk of food insecurity at any time.

Everyone's health is compromised by not having enough to eat, but the very young and the very old are the most vulnerable. A child who does not get enough nutrition, especially before the age of three, remains susceptible to a variety of health risks for the remainder of his or her life. A child's growth may be stunted — that child might not grow as tall or produce as much muscle mass as he or she would have with adequate nutrition as a baby. Such a child may also have a weakened immune system, which means he or she may get sick more often, and stay sick longer, than a child who received adequate nutrition. He or she may have cognitive problems, like difficulty paying attention, learning in school, and doing well on exams. A child that suffers early malnourishment may have behavior problems, which could also lead to problems in school.

Senior citizens are also vulnerable to food insecurity. As our bodies age, we need adequate nutrition to maintain a healthy lifestyle. Many of society's oldest citizens are no longer employed and may live on a fixed income. This income, which is usually lower than what they earned when they worked, may not be enough to pay for all their necessities, such as food. Health problems like diabetes, high blood pressure, and circulatory and

Parents in developing countries can get help for malnourished children at UNICEF-supported feeding centers, like the one this Sudanese mother brought her young son to in Southern Darfur.

Homeless people not only have to worry about where their next meal is coming from, they also have to worry about finding a safe place to live. Many homeless people depend on the kindness of strangers for money to buy something to eat.

heart problems can result from not having enough to eat. Hunger can also cause mental problems like depression.

Charities and philanthropies are working to rid the world of hunger completely. What will a world without hunger be like? It will be a place where the root causes of hunger, like poverty and injustice, are no longer threats to human dignity. Governments will commit to the welfare of their people by instituting policies that ensure everyone receives enough food to live a healthy life. But people will be able to rely primarily on their own resources for food and nutrition because they will have the knowledge, skills, and support needed to obtain enough food. This applies to those who grow their own food as well as those who get it from other sources. In other words, a world without hunger is a world where every person, regardless of where they live, their nationality, their age, or their income level, will have access to quality food of good nutritional value. A world without hunger is within our reach. And charities and philanthropies dedicated to ending hunger will continue to work tirelessly until every person on Earth has enough nutritious food to eat.

You Can Help, Too!

Now that you have read this book and learned of the many ways philanthropies and charities are working to improve the lives of those threatened by hunger, you may be wondering how you can help. Can one person really make a difference in such a huge problem? The answer is yes. In the back of this book you will find several ways that you can help alleviate hunger both in your neighborhood and around the world. No action is too small when it comes to eliminating hunger.

The philanthropies mentioned in this book are just a few of the many worthwhile organizations that are tirelessly working on the quest to end world hunger. All of them depend on donations to continue their work. If you would like to donate money to a specific charity, it's best to check it out first. Websites like Charity Navigator (charitynavigator.org), or the Better Business Bureau (www.bbb.org) are good sources that you can use to find out how a charity uses the money it receives. Whether you give of your time or your money, you will be doing your part to end world hunger.

There are lots of ways young people can help in the quest to end world hunger. Many people taking small steps can make a big difference.

WHAT YOU CAN DO TO HELP

Here are a few ways that you can participate in the quest to end world hunger:

Hold a bake sale at your school or place of worship. Donate the money raised to one of the philanthropies discussed in this book, or another organization you like.

Organize a canned food drive at your school, place of worship, or neighborhood. Donate what you collect to a local food bank or food pantry.

Find a local food bank in your community and volunteer your time sorting, stacking, or packing food to be distributed to those in need.

US programs that provide food aid to the poor are often at risk of being eliminated or reduced. Research the current issues, and write letters to members of Congress sharing your opinions on these issues. For example, you might ask your representative not to cut aid to the poor, especially aid that has to do with hunger, like the Supplemental Nutrition Assistance Program (SNAP).

Visit The Hunger Site at http://www.thehungersite.com. Clicking the orange box at the top of the page once a day provides food to needy people and costs you nothing.

CHAPTER NOTES

Full citations including web addresses can be found in Works Consulted.

Introduction

1. The Hunger Site, "World Leaders: End Hunger by 2015!"
2. Food and Agriculture Organization of the United Nations, "Food Security Indicators," December 20, 2013.
3. World Health Organization, "WHO Issues New Guidance for Treating Children with Severe Acute Malnutrition," November 27, 2013.
4. World Food Programme, "About."
5. World Food Programme, *Hunger*, "What Causes Hunger?"
6. Food and Agricultural Organization of the United Nations, *The State of Food Insecurity in the World 2013*, "The Multiple Dimensions of Food Security."
7. United Nations, Millenium Development Goals and Beyond 2015, "Goal 1: Eradicate Extreme Poverty & Hunger."
8. Food and Agricultural Organization of the United Nations, *The State of Food Insecurity in the World 2013*, "Executive Summary."

Chapter 1: Hunger in the United States

1. This story is based on a compilation of stories heard during the author's many years as a volunteer in a homeless shelter and soup kitchen. The name of the child has been fabricated and does not reflect the actual name of any of the children interviewed.
2. Alisha Coleman-Jensen, Mark Nord, and Anita Singh, United States Department of Agriculture, "Household Food Security in the United States in 2012," September 2013.
3. Feeding America, "The Emergency Food Assistance Program (TEFAP)."
4. Feeding America, "Commodity Supplemental Food Program (CSFP)."
5. Feeding America, "How Our Network Works."
6. Share Our Strength, No Kid Hungry, "About Us."
7. YMCA of the USA, "The Y Kicks off Food Program to Serve 4 Million," June 4, 2013.
8. Share Our Strength, No Kid Hungry, "Our Partners,"
9. YMCA of the USA, "The Y Kicks off Food Program to Serve 4 Million," June 4, 2013.
10. Feeding America, *Solving Hunger Together: 2013 Annual Report*, p. 9.

Chapter 2: Fighting Famine

1. Cormac Ó Gráda, *Famine: A Short History* (Princeton, NJ: Princeton University Press, 2009), p. 13.
2. Jim Donnelly, BBC, "The Irish Famine," February 17, 2011.
3. Save the Children, "One Year after Catastrophe: Still Saving Lives in East Africa."
4. Clare Mulley, HerStoria, "Eglantyne Jebb, 1876-1928, Founder of Save the Children and Champion of Children's Rights," August 19, 2012.
5. Save the Children, "Our History."
6. Ibid.
7. Enough Food for Everyone IF, "G8 Summit Briefing," April 2013.
8. Save the Children, "A Historic Moment in the Fight against Hunger," June 8, 2013.
9. Save the Children, "One Year after Catastrophe: Still Saving Lives in East Africa."
10. UNICEF, "Releasing Declining Numbers for Child Mortality, UNICEF Calls for Increased Efforts to Save Children's Lives," September 12, 2008.

Chapter 3: Helping Women Fight Hunger

1. The Hunger Project, "Our Results."
2. The Hunger Project, "Who We Are."
3. The Hunger Project, "Methodology."
4. The Hunger Project, "Empowering Women as Key Change Agents."
5. The Hunger Project, "Where We Work: South Asia."
6. Ibid.
7. The Hunger Project, "Microfinance Program: How It Works."
8. The Hunger Project, "Empowering Women as Key Change Agents."
9. Freedom from Hunger, "Credit with Education."
10. CARE, "History of CARE," October 15, 2013.

Chapter 4: Ending Hunger with Sustainable Agriculture

1. AGRA, "Our Story."
2. Ibid.
3. Freedom from Hunger, "Saving for Change."
4. Oxfam America, "Host an Oxfam America Hunger Banquet."
5. Farm Aid, "Farm Aid: Family Farmers, Good Food, a Better America."
6. Doctors Without Borders, "Malnutrition," May 2, 2013.
7. World Health Organization, "Malnutrition."

FURTHER READING

Books

Barker, Geoff. *Hunger*. Mankato, MN: Smart Apple Media, 2010.

Gay, Kathlyn. *Food: The New Gold*. Minneapolis: Twenty-First Century Books, 2013.

Kamberg, Mary-Lane. *Bono: Fighting World Hunger and Poverty*. New York: Rosen Publishing Company, 2009.

Rooney, Anne. *Feeding the World*. Mankato, MN: Smart Apple Media, 2010.

Walpole, Brenda. *Food for Everyone*. Mankato: MN: Sea-to-Sea Publications, 2010.

On the Internet

30 Hour Famine: Learn about how you can help make others aware of poverty in the world http://30hourfamine.org/

Free Rice: Play games to donate rice through the World Food Programme http://freerice.com/

World Food Day—October 16: Learn about ways you can participate http://www.worldfooddayusa.org/

World Food Programme http://www.wfp.org/

Works Consulted

AGRA. http://www.agra.org/

AGRA. "Our Story." http://www.agra.org/who-we-are/our-story/#.U1bgYvldWSo

CARE. http://www.care.org/

CARE. "History of CARE." October 15, 2013. http://www.care.org/impact/our-stories/care-history

Coleman-Jensen, Alisha, Mark Nord, and Anita Singh. "Household Food Security in the United States in 2012." United States Department of Agriculture, September 2013. http://www.ers.usda.gov/ersDownloadHandler.ashx?file=/media/1183208/err-155.pdf

Doctors Without Borders. "Malnutrition." May 2, 2013. http://www.doctorswithoutborders.org/our-work/medical-issues/malnutrition

Donnelly, Jim. "The Irish Famine." BBC, February 17, 2011. http://www.bbc.co.uk/history/british/victorians/famine_01.shtml

Enough Food for Everyone IF. "G8 Summit Briefing." April 2013. http://enoughfoodif.org/g8/briefing

Farm Aid. http://www.farmaid.org/

Farm Aid. "Farm Aid: Family Farmers, Good Food, a Better America." http://www.farmaid.org/site/c.qlI5IhNVJsE/b.2723609/k.C8F1/About_Us.htm

Feeding America. "Child Hunger Facts." http://feedingamerica.org/hunger-in-america/hunger-facts/child-hunger-facts.aspx

Feeding America. "Commodity Supplemental Food Program (CSFP)." http://feedingamerica.org/how-we-fight-hunger/advocacy-public-policy/policy-center/federal-anti-hunger-programs-and-policies/commodity-supplemental-food-program.aspx

Feeding America. "How Our Network Works." http://feedingamerica.org/how-we-fight-hunger/our-food-bank-network/how-our-network-works.aspx

Feeding America. "Hunger & Poverty Statistics." http://feedingamerica.org/hunger-in-america/hunger-facts/hunger-and-poverty-statistics.aspx

Feeding America. "Impact of Hunger." http://feedingamerica.org/hunger-in-america/impact-of-hunger.aspx

Feeding America. *Solving Hunger Together: 2013 Annual Report*. p. 9. http://feedingamerica.org/how-we-fight-hunger/about-us/~/media/Files/financial/FeedingAmericaAnnualReport2013_SolvingHungerTogether.ashx

Feeding America. "The Emergency Food Assistance Program (TEFAP)." http://feedingamerica.org/how-we-fight-hunger/advocacy-public-policy/policy-center/federal-anti-hunger-programs-and-policies/the-emergency-food-assistance-program.aspx

Food and Agriculture Organization of the United Nations. "Executive Summary." *The State of Food Insecurity in the World 2013*. http://www.fao.org/docrep/018/i3458e/i3458e.pdf

Food and Agriculture Organization of the United Nations. "Food Security Indicators." December 20, 2013. http://bit.ly/14FRxGV

Food and Agriculture Organization of the United Nations. "The Multiple Dimensions of Food Security." *The State of Food Insecurity in the World 2013*. http://www.fao.org/publications/SOFI/en/

Food and Agriculture Organization of the United Nations. *The State of Food Insecurity in the World 2012*. Rome: FAO, 2012. http://www.fao.org/docrep/016/i3027e/i3027e.pdf

Freedom from Hunger. http://www.freedomfromhunger.org/

Freedom from Hunger. "Credit with Education." https://www.freedomfromhunger.org/credit-education

Freedom from Hunger. "Saving for Change." https://www.freedomfromhunger.org/saving-change

The History Place. "Irish Potato Famine." http://www.historyplace.com/worldhistory/famine/introduction.htm

The Hunger Project. http://www.thp.org/

The Hunger Project. "Empowering Women as Key Change Agents." http://www.thp.org/what_we_do/program_overview/empowering_women

The Hunger Project. "Methodology." http://www.thp.org/what_we_do/program_overview/methodology

The Hunger Project. "Microfinance Program: How It Works." http://www.thp.org/what_we_do/key_initiatives/microfinance/how_it_works

44

FURTHER READING

The Hunger Project. "Our Results." http://www.thp.org/see_our_results

The Hunger Project. "Where We Work: South Asia." http://www.thp.org/where_we_work/south_asia

The Hunger Project. "Who We Are." http://www.thp.org/who_we_are

The Hunger Site. http://www.thehungersite.com/

The Hunger Site. "World Leaders: End Hunger by 2015!" http://thehungersite.greatergood.com/clickToGive/ths/petition/G8SummitHunger

Jyoti, Diana F., Edward A. Frongillo, and Sonya J. Jones. "Food Insecurity Affects School Children's Academic Performance, Weight Gain, and Social Skills." *Journal of Nutrition,* December 1, 2005, vol. 135, no. 12, pp. 2831–2839.

Kleinman, Ronald E., et. al. "Hunger in Children in the United States: Potential Behavioral and Emotional Correlates." *Pediatrics,* January 1, 1998, vol. 101, no. 1.

McGovern, George. *The Third Freedom: Ending Hunger in Our Time.* New York: Simon & Shuster, 2001.

Mulley, Clare. "Eglantyne Jebb, 1876-1928, Founder of Save the Children and Champion of Children's Rights." HerStoria, August 19, 2012. http://herstoria.com/?p=663

Ó Gráda, Cormac. *Famine: A Short History.* Princeton, NJ: Princeton University Press, 2009.

Oxfam America. http://www.oxfamamerica.org

Oxfam America. "Host an Oxfam America Hunger Banquet." http://www.oxfamamerica.org/take-action/events/hunger-banquet/

Oxfam International. http://www.oxfam.org/

Russell, Sharman Apt. *Hunger: An Unnatural History.* New York: Perseus, 2005.

Save the Children. http://www.savethechildren.org/

Save the Children. "A Historic Moment in the Fight against Hunger." June 8, 2013. http://www.savethechildren.org.uk/news-and-comment/news/2013-07/historic-moment-fight-against-hunger

Save the Children. "One Year after Catastrophe: Still Saving Lives in East Africa." http://savethechildren.org.nz/assets/620/East%20Africa%201%20Year%20On%20Report%20FINAL_for%20web.pdf

Save the Children. "Our History." http://www.savethechildren.org.uk/about-us/history

Schwartz-Nobel, Loretta. *Growing Up Empty.* New York: HarperCollins, 2002.

Share Our Strength. "About Us." No Kid Hungry. https://www.nokidhungry.org/about-us

Share Our Strength. No Kid Hungry. http://www.nokidhungry.org/

Share Our Strength. "Our Partners." No Kid Hungry. http://www.nokidhungry.org/partners

Slack, Kristen S. and Joan Yoo. "Food Hardship and Child Behavior Problems among Low-Income Children." *Social Service Review,* January 2005, vol. 79, issue 3, pp. 511–536.

Stanford, Claire, ed. *World Hunger.* Bronx, NY: The H.W. Wilson Company, 2007.

UNICEF. "Releasing Declining Numbers for Child Mortality, UNICEF Calls for Increased Efforts to Save Children's Lives." September 12, 2008. http://www.unicef.org/media/media_45607.html

UNICEF United States Fund. http://www.unicefusa.org/

United Nations. Millenium Development Goals and Beyond 2015. "Goal 1: Eradicate Extreme Poverty & Hunger." http://www.un.org/millenniumgoals/poverty.shtml

United States Census Bureau. "International Programs." http://www.census.gov/population/international/

United States Department of Agriculture, Food and Nutrition Service. "Commodity Supplemental Food Program (CSFP)." March 10, 2014. http://www.fns.usda.gov/csfp/commodity-supplemental-food-program-csfp

World Food Programme. "About." http://www.wfp.org/about

World Food Programme. *Hunger.* "FAQs." http://www.wfp.org/hunger/faqs

World Food Programme. *Hunger.* "What Causes Hunger?" http://www.wfp.org/hunger/causes

World Health Organization. "Malnutrition." http://www.who.int/maternal_child_adolescent/topics/child/malnutrition/en/

World Health Organization. "Nutrition." http://www.who.int/nutrition

World Health Organization. "WHO Issues New Guidance for Treating Children with Severe Acute Malnutrition." November 27, 2013. http://www.who.int/mediacentre/news/notes/2013/severe-acute-malnutrition-20131127/en/

YMCA of the USA. "The Y Kicks off Food Program to Serve 4 Million." June 4, 2013. http://www.ymca.net/news-releases/y-kicks-off-summer-food-program-to-serve-4-million-meals-to-kids-nationwide

GLOSSARY

advocacy (AD-vuh-kuh-see)—The act of supporting or speaking up for a cause.

affiliation (uh-fil-ee-EY-shuhn)—Being associated or connected with something.

allocation (al-uh-KEY-shuhn)—A share or portion that is reserved for a specific person, group, or purpose.

arable (AR-uh-buhl)—Able to be used to grow crops.

calorie (KAL-uh-ree)—A unit for measuring energy from food.

cognitive (KOG-ni-tiv)—Related to the mental process of knowing or understanding something.

compromised (KOM-pruh-mahyzd)—Not able to function properly because of disease or other conditions.

developing country—A country whose economy is based on farming as opposed to industry, leading to a lower standard of living.

domestic (duh-MES-tik)—Pertaining to one's own home or country.

eradicate (ih-RAD-i-keyt)—To remove or eliminate completely.

famine (FAM-in)—A severe shortage of food that puts a population at risk of starvation.

fixed income—An amount of money received regularly that doesn't change over time.

food pantry—A place that distributes nonperishable foods, like canned goods, to people who need them.

grassroots—Led by ordinary people.

humanitarian (hyoo-man-i-TAIR-ee-uhn)—Related to the happiness or well-being of people.

implementation (im-pluh-muhn-TEY-shuhn)—The act of putting something into effect.

interest rate—A percentage of additional money that is paid back when money is borrowed.

investment—The money that is put to use to purchase goods or services that will generate or increase profits.

microfinance—A nontraditional way of providing a small loan for the purpose of starting a business, usually to a poor person who has nothing to use as collateral.

mortality (mawr-TAL-i-tee)—Death.

poverty (POV-er-tee)—The condition of having little or no money or material possessions.

standard of living—A level of comfort (or lack thereof) enjoyed by a community or family.

starvation (stahr-VEY-shuhn)—The condition of death or dying caused by malnourishment.

sub-Saharan (suhb-suh-HAR-uhn)—Related to the part of Africa that is south of the Sahara Desert.

INDEX

ABOUT THE AUTHOR

Marylou Morano Kjelle is a college English professor, freelance writer, and photojournalist who lives and works in Central New Jersey. Marylou has written dozens of books for young readers of all ages. She holds MS and MA degrees from Rutgers University, where she also teaches children's writing. When not teaching or writing, Marylou gardens, cooks, and bakes for her family and friends, watches movies, and reads as many books as she possibly can.